Words, Wonder, and the Divine in You

# Words, Wonder, and the Divine in You

**by the Rev. Dr. Deborah Roof**

Peter E. Randall Publisher
Portsmouth, New Hampshire
2023

ISBN print: 978-1-942155-65-2
ISBN eBook: 978-1-942155-66-9
Library of Congress Control Number: 2023914060

Published by
Peter E. Randall Publisher
5 Greenleaf Woods Drive, Unit 102
Portsmouth, NH 03801

Text design by Tim Holtz
Cover design by Janet Bagley
Author photo credit: John Noltner, "A Peace of My Mind"

Printed in the United States

To my amazing daughters, Stephanie and Brittany, of whom I am so very proud, and to my wife, Liz, who is proof of the Divine.

# Contents

# Who Am I?

Our journeys are what make this physical life so interesting. This book is a recounting of how spirituality has led me and fed me. My prayer is that recounting my experiences may lead you to begin to ponder your own journey and perhaps be kinder to yourself for not knowing what you didn't know.

Are we physical beings having a spiritual experience or are we spiritual beings having a physical experience? That is the question. We seek, we explore, and we yearn for meaning. Each of us has a story to tell and every one of us has a light and a gift to share. When we summon this energy within us, some call it "service"; others "call"; and others "destiny." I'll go one step further and call it "divinity." We are divinely created and within each one of us lies the magic of Spirit—a life force. Along the way, we fail, we falter, and we fall down. And that's okay. It's a journey—a wonder-filled and wonderful journey.

I am so passionate about the wonder that surrounds us! I wanted to create a forum where people might share their knowledge, their hope, and their mystical experiences with one another. I set down these pages in hopes of beginning a conversation, a sacred conversation. When we follow that urging to follow through on some crazy idea, we don't know where it will lead. So, we muster the energy and the courage and we move forward. Let's see where You lead, Holy One.

Don't get me wrong: writing a book is intimidating. And here's the thing: I always believed that there was a book inside me. I have no idea where this will lead me, and I know I've got to follow through. And then, we never know, do we?

You may not have read some of the authors I have read. Karoline M. Lewis, an author friend of mine, is one of the most brilliant biblical scholars and interpreters of the Gospel of John, yet just yesterday, I met someone who hasn't read her book yet. So, I know that we each need to share our golden nuggets of grace and hope with one another. I have learned a lot, and I want to share my story with people who may not have witnessed some of the things I have witnessed. I hope and pray that this is a kind of springboard to more writing, more conversations, and a deeper understanding of what it is to live this wonderful thing we call life.

My message is simple: we are more alike than we are different. Maya Angelou's exquisite poem *Human Family* claims this profound truth. The second piece of that divine truth is that we are all part of the same divine, universal energy. We are interconnected in amazing ways.

I grew up in the Christian tradition, and I became a Christian minister. In my church work and in my travels, I learned a variety of ways in which God expresses God's self. This includes those manifestations of the Divine that are not rooted in Christian experience and expression. I love the beauty and the wonder of those sixty-six sacred books assembled together into what we call the Bible. And I love poetry of all kinds. I appreciate the beauty and the wisdom that is found in other manifestations of spirituality. You will see the names of people who have guided my journey. I love them all and I am so grateful for each one.

The Christian tradition is a tradition filled with wonder. And I have always believed in a love that was greater than the human ability to express it. When you pay close attention to many of the words of scripture, there is an overarching human condition which is enduring and beyond any one religion. In fact, those same words may even be archetypal. In other words, they may be timeless.

That said, much of the beauty of the Christian tradition has been clouded by institutional trappings, by rules and laws, and by *shoulds* and *shouldn'ts*. I choose the wonder and the beauty that avails itself within the tradition over any rigid, outward form.

Parts I and II of this book address how the words we use matter and how the wonder that surrounds us matters. In Part III, I take the traditional Christian trinity concept and stretch it out a bit—or a lot, for some people. Stretching too much can be off-putting. I understand that. My overarching concept is to take God out of the box we have created while still acknowledging an understanding of the gifts of that box, if possible.

In these pages, I have shared specific scriptural references from the Bible, as well as references to other spiritual leaders, philosophers and wisdom teachers outside the Christian tradition who have influenced my pondering. You will even read an occasional reference to a truth found in science fiction—one of the culturally accepted milieu for people who imagine and envision alternative ways of being in the universe. Star Trek, for example, expresses a theology that encompasses all life forms and the good that we can do as we seek to serve sentient beings—no matter what galaxy they live in.

People have asked me who my audience is for this book. The truth is that I know I am writing this book for me. I also believe that there are people who crave meaning as much as I do. Perhaps there are people who wonder if there isn't more to be said and learned about spirituality. These people may enjoy reading my offering. Perhaps someone who has been hurt by organized religion may find a healing balm in these pages. Meaning and healing often go hand in hand. I do know this: this book is not for people who want proof of something. I have no proof. I can only offer my experience.

Bountiful blessings!

## PART I

# Words Matter:
# Watch Your Language

*"If we understood the power of our thoughts, we would guard them more closely. If we understood the awesome power of our words, we would prefer silence to almost anything negative. In our thoughts and words, we create our own weaknesses and our own strengths. Our limitations and joys begin in our hearts. We can always replace negative with positive."*

—Betty Eadie

"In the beginning . . ."[1]

True story: There is a statue of the Buddha in Thailand that was thought to be built of unremarkable materials. While some people were attempting to move it in the mid-twentieth century, they damaged the outer coating, which then revealed a golden glint coming from underneath. Layers of clay, mud, and pieces of broken glass were carefully removed only to reveal a magnificent statue of solid gold! No one knows for sure how the golden statue came to be hidden within this commonplace shell, but theories have emerged based on its location and the history of the area. Centuries ago, much of the country was under siege. Temples were being destroyed and all forms of gold, including the golden statues of the Buddha, were stolen and carried away to be melted down. The monks who were watching over this particular Buddha must have had the idea of covering it with clay,

---

1   The first book in the Old Testament and the Gospel of John in the New Testament both begin with these simple words. I claim the ancient wisdom of "in the beginning" as I begin to share the testament which is the testimony of my Spirit. All biblical references in this book come from *The Discipleship Study Bible: New Revised Standard Version including Apocrypha*, Westminster John Knox Press, 2008.

mud, and pieces of glass to hide its true value. The metaphor of the muddy Buddha is a perfect image for anyone courageous enough to reclaim the "gold" that is our true nature.

In the second letter to the Corinthians in the New Testament, the Apostle Paul writes, "We have this treasure in clay jars, so that it may be made clear that this extraordinary power belongs to God and does not come from us." A master of metaphor, the Apostle Paul's reference to "clay jars" refers to this physical body we inhabit during our lifetimes.[2] The "extraordinary power" is the light/Spirit of God within us. It is a treasure beyond our comprehension. It is the golden Buddha inside each one of us, calling to us—and calling upon us—to embrace our true nature.

We are light. We are not our mistakes; we can learn from them. We are pure light inside some flesh and bones. The more we concentrate on this light—disregarding anything that is not light—the closer we come to the divinity that is our true nature. The

---

2  Genesis 2:7 (New Revised Standard Version [NRSV]): "[T]hen the LORD God formed man from the dust of the ground and breathed into his nostrils the breath of life; and the man became a living being."

Apostle Paul wrote in his letter to the Philippians (4:8): "Finally, beloved, whatever is true, whatever is honorable, whatever is just, whatever is pure, whatever is pleasing, whatever is commendable, if there is any excellence and if there is anything worthy of praise, think about these things." We accomplish this potential only by accepting and embracing our true self and our inner light.

In the same way, we are Spirit—connected and connecting to all Spirit which is in all life forms. That Spirit is divine. Divinity surrounds us. The more we are in touch with it, the more it reveals itself to us. As creations, we are limited by our physical existence and our particular language. The Divine is limitless. The Divine speaks every language and appears in every culture. Not only does the Divine surround us, the Divine also dwells within us. The more we pay attention to this in-dwelling Presence of Abundance, the easier it will be to perceive Divine-Presence in our midst.

When I was in college, I spent my junior year studying at the Sorbonne in Paris, spending vacations in

Germany, and I became a student of languages. The year following my graduation from college, I spent another year teaching English in a high school in Mayenne, France. Speaking other languages, teaching English to non-English speakers, and traveling abroad gave me a keen respect for language and for words. In my later years, studying the Bible, I learned that what we read and call "gospel" is the translation of a translation of a translation of words from a culture that no longer exists. Language mirrors the culture in which it is spoken. These are not unimportant distinctions.

For the sake of this book, I am suggesting three realms that matter to me right here and right now: Words matter. Wonder matters. Spirituality matters. My approach to articulating this perspective relates directly to seeking meaning and uncovering value in our midst. The way we talk reflects what we believe to be true.

It does not "go without saying." Too often we cut corners because we believe that we have said enough. When we know what we mean, we cut corners— sometimes unintentionally—resulting in misunderstanding. There are messages that we need to say and we need to hear. Messages like: You matter. Your energy matters. Your life matters. Your light matters.

In the fable by Antoine de Saint-Exupéry, *The Little Prince*, the fox tells the little prince that "Words are the source of misunderstanding." Whereas his point may have been that actions speak louder than words, the fact is that language, which is essentially a combination of words, is the only implement that we possess to deliver meaning and provide understanding. We have developed languages to better communicate and to express our thoughts and emotions. And because we are essentially poetic creations, we have the tools of metaphor and simile and poetry of all incarnations to help convey our thoughts and help us get our point across to others.

I become concerned, however, when people underestimate the influence that language has on our society. Language can build bridges or build walls. With our extensive yet finite vocabulary, humans have tried to articulate the mysterious and unpack the unexplainable. We have tried and failed to accomplish the task because the mysterious defies explanation. And we still try. We must try. We get closer to understanding and closer to one another. That is, until we don't. I have become increasingly motivated by my intention and my attention. I ask myself: what is my intention? I then pay attention to what I intend. And finally, I demand of myself that I pay attention to how I use words.

Words matter because they are so powerful. Words have the power to build up and the power to tear down. They have the ability to create and the power to destroy. Learning how to use words with attentive intention and being precise in our choice of vocabulary will help us to grow spiritually. A friend told me a story recently about something her mother used to say. She said: "Your body knows what your mouth is saying." What we say resonates in our body. The words we choose to use are recorded in our being. This is a powerful truth.

We need to pay attention to our context. Sometimes one particular word can mean one thing in one time and place and something else in a different time and place. I offer one illustration that is personal for me: the word "queer." I am a child of the '50s. And if you are, too, you may have even cringed as you read the word. The word *queer* was highly derogatory back then. It was an insult pure and simple. I came out as a same-gender-loving woman in 1994. At that time, I simply said that I realized I was *gay*. A few years after coming out, I noticed that the LGBT population had reclaimed the word *queer*. It's as if they took ownership of the word. And yes, there are some LGBTQIA+ folks today who prefer using all the letters. For others, *queer* has become a comfortable word—a reclaimed word that its own culture took back.

In parallel fashion, the word *God* may invoke negative feelings for people who have been hurt by organized religion. For them the word *God* causes distress. If this is the case for you, I understand and I beg your indulgence if you decide to continue reading. In my own context, Christian scripture was weaponized against me: A pastor who told me I wasn't normal, a denomination that would not ordain me, a denomination that would accept me if I didn't tell anyone who I truly was, churches that would not even interview me because of my sexual identity, Christians who tell me that they love me but hate my sin. Even recently, a guest pianist rescinded his offer to play for one of my worship services when he learned that I am married to a woman.

Perhaps you know this kind of prejudice, too. From the cross, Jesus said: "They know not what they do." This is still true today. People are afraid of what they do not understand and they often cling to the rules set down by others. The Pharisees were protecting what they believed to be sacred. The "gay averse" feel that they are protecting what they believe to be sacred. I don't think that they understand. God is bigger than the rules. Love is bigger than the rules. That was the point Jesus tried to make and they still put him to death.

I learned that God is not the church. I am able to see the difference and get past what was done to me "in the name of God." *They know not what they do.* My ultimate goal is to express Divinity to the best of my ability, all the while acknowledging that the act of describing or naming is reductionist. Divinity is always expanding. God has many names. Words matter.

In his book *The Four Agreements*, Don Miguel Ruiz calls his First Agreement: "Be impeccable with your word." What does this mean exactly? What does impeccability look like? Here are some clues: Say only what you mean. Speak with integrity. Avoid using words to speak negatively against yourself or to gossip about others.

Words are incredibly powerful. Word choice is equally poignant. Consider an explanation from the Old Testament. The book of Proverbs, chapter 15 explains:

<sup>1</sup> A soft answer turns away wrath,
   but a harsh word stirs up anger.
<sup>2</sup> The tongue of the wise dispenses knowledge,
   but the mouths of fools pour out folly . . .
<sup>4</sup> A gentle tongue is a tree of life,
   but perverseness in it breaks the spirit.

Words do all of what this writer describes. They turn away rage and dispense information. A tree of life thrives in gentle spirit and gentle expression. When words are soft, wise, and gentle our spirits thrive. However, words used harshly stir up resentment, thoughtlessness pours out foolishness, and perverseness can actually break one's spirit.

In his book *The Hidden Messages in Water*, Dr. Masaru Emoto conducted a variety of studies using frozen water crystals. He used different kinds of water and also exposed different water specimens to both affirming and discouraging verbal messages. He took photographs showing how water reacts differently depending upon its makeup and the messages to which it is exposed. Water from clear springs and water that has been exposed to loving words or kind messages looked noticeably different from polluted water or water exposed to negative messages. Upon examining the photographs of these frozen water crystals, clean water and water exposed to positive messages showed brilliant, complex, and colorful snowflake patterns. In contrast, crystals of polluted water or water exposed to negative messaging were almost incomplete, with asymmetrical patterns and dull colors. Emoto's conclusion demonstrated the power of our words using these frozen water crystals as his gauge. He and his assistants would repeatedly say "thank you" in the presence of this water and the frozen crystals of water were stunning and beautiful. When they would say something negative, the frozen crystals of water were murky and appeared polluted.

Dr. Emoto's conclusion was that our words have power. What if we take his research one step farther and consider that we are, after all, 70 percent water? It is a logical conclusion that we, therefore, respond positively to affirming messages of love and gratitude, just as we respond to negative messages by absorbing the negativity. Would you agree?

Words matter.

# CHAPTER 1

# *And* Rather Than *But*
## Words matter

When I listen to a person's use of words—and I am truly listening—I try to hear the speaker's choice of words. One word, one phrase can be quite revealing. I hear someone working in the other room. I hear them say under their breath, "Oh, I'm such an idiot!" This negative self-talk is extremely detrimental to one's own sense of self-worth and it disobeys the greatest commandment that Jesus taught: to love oneself.[1] And since it was so spontaneous on the speaker's part, it feels clear to me that they often talk badly to themself about themself.

Sometimes a person quite inadvertently contradicts themself, without intending to do so. A child might say casually in conversation, "Daddy doesn't

---

[1]  Known as the "Greatest Commandment" (love God, love neighbor as yourself), it appears in the Gospels of Matthew (22:35–40), Mark (12:28–31) and Luke (10:25–28), as well as in the Old Testament, in Leviticus (19:18).

get mad all the time." Without meaning to, and most likely in hopes of protecting his father, the child is actually confessing that Daddy does get mad on occasion and that it is pretty uncomfortable. Or a wife who comes for counseling is trying to make the best of a bad situation and says without realizing what she's saying, "But he doesn't hit me much." The listener has learned that, in fact, her husband beats her. It's all about one's intention and paying attention—for the speaker and for the listener.

Words matter. Even the three-letter words like *and* and *but*. We choose particular words—sometimes intentionally, sometimes unintentionally, and sometimes out of habit. The unfortunate reality about habit is that we may not be paying much attention at all.

There's an expression in addiction recovery circles: "Everything before the word *but* is malarkey [that is, meaningless talk; nonsense]."[2] I heard that and thought: "Really? Could this be true?" Could it possibly be accurate that whenever you say "but" you are

---

2 The actual expression is "horse sh*t." I just didn't want to be profane in my first book.

disregarding or discounting the words that preceded it? Do you mean that the idea expressed first is somehow "less than" or untrue or otherwise unimportant? And perhaps even *malarkey*?

Consider some examples: "The weather is beautiful, *but* there's a storm coming in." Where is the emphasis? On the storm! The current beautiful weather of the here and now is upstaged by a storm in the future. "He is a great dad *but* he beats mom." How great a dad can he be if he is beating their mother? The current greatness of the dad is overshadowed by those occasions when he is not so great. "Jesus says to love everybody *but* I just don't think I can love Harry." So, even though Jesus says "everybody," the speaker cannot bring themself to accomplish it. The use of *but* demonstrates knowing and defying what Jesus commanded.

One of the most pervasive behaviors in our society today is the cultural norm of wanting more than we currently have. It is so prevalent that we don't even think that we are ever enough. We don't feel good enough. In school, we don't feel smart enough. In business, we aren't successful enough. We want more.

We don't have enough money. We don't have enough clothing. You name it! This affects our self-image and our self-confidence. "I'm not pretty enough." "I'm just not good enough."

What if we could reconcile our feelings with what culture dictates just by changing one word? What if we could replace *but* with *and?* "I am enough *and* sometimes I feel that I could be so much more." Both are true. "I know I studied really hard for that test" or "I know that I prepared really well for that interview—and I didn't do as well as I had hoped." Both halves of the sentence are true! You didn't get the results that you wanted and it doesn't change the reality that you did work toward that goal. Using the word *but* casts a negative shadow to the first component.

*And* is like addition. *But* is like subtraction. Jesus did say to love *everyone.* I try and I will keep trying. It doesn't make me a loser that I am not able to do it all the time—yet.

Notice in the verses from Proverbs 15 that I cited previously that each verse used *but.* Notice the order. In most cases, there was something positive, followed by *but*, followed by something negative. How different would the feeling invoked by these verses be if all these *buts* were *and*?

¹ A soft answer turns away wrath,
[and] a harsh word stirs up anger.
² The tongue of the wise dispenses knowledge,
[and] the mouths of fools pour out folly . . .
⁴ A gentle tongue is a tree of life,
[and] perverseness in it breaks the spirit.

Did you feel the difference? The two halves are equal rather than one being subordinate to the other. You know how on TV they say, "Don't try this at home"? That is not the case here. I do encourage you to try this as much as you can. You will begin to see things differently and feel the discord that the word *but* inherently carries within it. You may, in fact, begin to notice that many times *and* is more accurate than *but*.

The more we shift to using *and* rather than *but* the more we will accept things as they are—which is a very healthy way to be in the world today. There is peace in acceptance. Early twentieth-century pastor and theologian Reinhold Niebuhr penned the "Serenity Prayer":

> *God, grant me the serenity to accept the things I cannot change, the courage to change the things I can, and the wisdom to know the difference.*

There are no *buts* in this prayer. It is a prayer full of empowerment and full of *and*s. All of these truths co-exist.

Choosing to use *and* instead of *but* is a small change that will make a big difference in your mindset and in your life. Listen to yourself and the next time you want to say *but*, try to say *and* instead. This tiny shift opens you up to a world of possibilities!

# CHAPTER 2

# *Either ... Or*
# Words matter

The words that we use to articulate our reality often shape our reality. Pretty soon, our reality is being shaped by the words we use. We have become a binary society in so many ways. One expression that mirrors this mindset more than many others is "either ... or." This point of view or worldview has subtly become so much a part of our language that it has contributed to a divisiveness that feeds current cultural division.

Every culture develops norms. It is real. These norms are sometimes articulated and sometimes insinuated. An *either ... or* worldview is one current cultural norm in our country that is extremely unhealthy. It is a binary perception that you are *either* with me *or* against me. It is destructive and dangerous. We start to believe that people are *either* one thing *or* another. They are honest *or* they are liars. They are introvert *or* extrovert. They are conservative *or* liberal. They are pro-progress *or* pro-environment.

Sadly, these *either . . . or* scenarios contribute to a deepening polarity. One cultural and political hot button issue is the *either . . . or* scenario of pro-life and pro-choice. Both movements took on lives of their own after the 1973 U.S. Supreme Court ruling of Roe vs. Wade. This was not a new tug-of-war. This argument about abortion has been around for a very long time. In the '70s, the wordsmiths and PR policy spinners determined that the term *pro-life* sounded less negative than *anti-abortion*. Fast forward fifty-plus years and here's the thing: many pro-life political advocates do not consistently vote on issues that are in fact "pro" life. For example, there is a severe lack of funding for early childhood programs, for nutrition programs for the food insecure, for foster care programs, and the list goes on. Pro-life advocates do not consistently vote in favor of these quality-of-life programs and these advocates for life do not always favor the life of the woman carrying the fetus. Are they *pro* the mother's life?

One health organization that has fallen victim to this *either . . . or* worldview is Planned Parenthood. This organization spends a fraction of its total budget on abortion care (3%).[1] The blind hatred for the organization by pro-life advocates is difficult to understand. The majority of funding at Planned Parenthood provides education and care. It offers women's health services and prenatal care. Without a doubt, Planned Parenthood has become a casualty of our divisive *either . . . or* thinking.

As a pastor, I have seen churches lose members because of *either . . . or* thinking. One member of the church supports "Black Lives Matter." The minister doesn't take a side. Another member, who does not approve of the spending policies of the national Black Lives Matter movement, leaves the church saying: "I can't support a church who thinks that's okay." The reality is that the church does not "think it's okay." The church doesn't take a stand because the minister of the church doesn't want to be in the middle of a

---

1   Ezra Klein, *Washington Post*, "Repost: What Planned Parenthood actually does, in one chart," February 2, 2012.

no-win *either . . . or* standoff. In this case, not taking a stand is perceived as taking a stand and the church loses a member.

Modernity did not invent *either . . . or* thinking and the Bible didn't exclude God from this worldview. The Bible portrays God as an *either . . . or* God right at the beginning. "Don't eat that fruit or you'll die."[2] Stories like this one reflect the writer and the context of the people rather than God. The Bible contains stories of judgment and stories of overwhelming compassion. The stories of compassion often surprise onlookers. Abraham's wife, Sarah, had a maid servant, named Hagar, who gave birth to Abraham's son—at Sarah's request. Sarah grew to hate the woman and the boy. She told Abraham to cast them out, which he did. He left them in the desert to die. God appeared to Hagar and saved both her and her son.[3]

Which is easier to believe? God is forgiving? Or God is judging? God is loving? Or God is punishing?

---

2   Genesis 2:1: "but of the tree of the knowledge of good and evil you shall not eat, for in the day you eat of it you shall die."

3   Genesis 21: 8–20. The story of the birth of Islam.

Your image of God may be a reflection of the church who taught you rather than who God is. Are stories of a judging God easier to believe than stories of redemption and forgiveness? And is this a reflection of how comfortable we are with a stern deity? We need to wonder whether we are creating a God that makes sense to us, a God who is created in our own image. We then might wonder if that is what the ancients did while writing those books of the Old Testament.

There are a multitude of examples of how *either . . . or* thinking has caused more harm than good. What's the answer? Is there one? I wonder if we could promote paying attention and trying not to fall victim to cultural metaphors that are perhaps used out of habit rather than purposeful intention. Think about it. If you believe something, is your choice of vocabulary in harmony with your belief? You may think so. I know I thought so. I thought that my words must reflect what I believed until I paid attention and asked myself the question: Does my language, that is, my choice of words, reveal or betray my beliefs? My answer is "not always."

Recently, I noticed a chilling example of the power of word choice in my own speech. I do not like violence of any kind. I don't like violence in movies. I don't like violence in relationships. I question the necessity of violence. And then I noticed something. In our everyday language, there are countless expressions that are violent in nature or in origin. Even when violence is not the intended outcome, we use militaristic or violent metaphors with disturbing ease. Here is an example. Like many folks, I pray for peace. I pray for the "peace that passes all human understanding." And then I hear myself say, "We need to *fight* for peace." I'm sorry—what? Why do I say *fight* for peace? People say it all the time. It's a habit and we aren't paying attention.

Another example that we use out of habit is "kill." "I would *kill* for a peanut butter sundae right now." Wait. What? Or when something occurs to me spontaneously, I might say that something just *"hit me up side the head."* Really? Another example: I heard a public official instructing his staff to listen closely to how people speak. He then went on to say that listening to someone's choice of words and then using that person's own words back in your response "will give you the *ammo* you need" to make your point. "Ammo"? Where are all these violent expressions coming from? I happen to know that this public official is against all gun violence and doesn't promote violence in any form, either. So, how is it that using the word "ammo" is automatic when a word like "tool" would work just as nicely? These are the kinds of word choices that I try to pay attention to.

Author and management consultant Margaret Wheatley has worked for more than forty years as a consultant, speaker, writer, teacher, and poet. She is known for bringing a diversified, cross-cultural per-spective to leadership, systems, and organizations, also bringing along the sense of value in building relation-ships and being of service to the greater community. Wheatley often suggests that being curious can move us from an extreme viewpoint. It helps if one can be humble, she also suggests.

Shifting us to center leads us away from *either . . . or*, which is neither humble nor curious, and one of the reasons why I find such value and beauty in the act of wondering, as discussed later in this book.

# CHAPTER 3

# *Both . . . And*
# Words matter

One of the wisest things I ever heard was "both are true." What?! That's crazy talk! BOTH are true?! How could that be? Both can't be true! Or can they? And I discovered that both can indeed be true.

As a parent, I love my children with all my heart *and* I can wish that they would make different choices. Loving does not mean agreeing with everything. And disagreement does not need to lead to divisiveness or division.

As a pastor, I was first introduced to *both . . . and* in my work with grieving families. In moments of grief, we feel enormous sadness that our loved one is gone, *and* we may also feel enormous relief that their suffering is over. Almost simultaneously, we cry because our loved one is dead *and* we laugh at something silly that they did. *Both* can be true.

The more I paid attention to the wonder of God's creation and the more I refrained from my own dangerous divisive thinking (a.k.a. *either . . . or*), the more I came to recognize that many times *both* can be true. Let's take a look at some benign examples. I might look fantastic in this black dress *and* I hate to wear it because I don't like how it makes me feel on the inside. Perhaps my daughter lost the really important soccer game *and* she played really well and is proud of her performance. I may prefer days filled with sunshine *and* Mother Earth really needs a long drink of water in the form of rain right about now.

We have a *both . . . and* God, for example. Jesus lived and showed loving grace to everyone he met, teaching and modeling what that grace looks like. *And* Jesus died because people feared this unusual behavior more than they could put into words. Fear causes anxiety and fear makes people do harsh things, hurtful things. God is a God of love and doesn't interfere with our day-to-day decisions. God grieves in our tragedy and rejoices in our success. Both are true.

There are some current cultural issues that are not benign. Someone who is pro-life can also support the death penalty. Someone who is pro-choice would never get an abortion. A Democrat can support the honest and integrity-filled Republican, just as easily as a Republican can support an honest and integrity-filled Democrat. In a world that appears to be conniving to split us down the middle, we do not have to submit and fall in step with contentious cultural behavior. We can disagree without becoming violent. We can face conflict with openness to the beloved other's point of view.

The book of Ecclesiastes 1:9 says, "What has been is what will be, and what has been done is what will be done; *there is nothing new under the sun.*" Original ideas are not always unique to our current time and place. Great ideas happen all the time and throughout time. Leonardo da Vinci made drawings of flying machines long before the technology had caught up to the idea. Sometimes great ideas happen on different continents at the same time. There is a good chance that someone has already said that beautiful pearl of wisdom that you just thought up. Biologists call it "parallel evolution" when it happens in nature. It happens in human creativity, which is connected to nature, all the time.

In my personal experience, there were occasions when I thought of something that I believed to be brand new, maybe even radical, only to discover that there was already a book on the subject. The first time I recognized this phenomenon was in the early '90s. A monumental truth had occurred to me and I wanted to write a book. I wanted to explain this truth that I imagined was a game-changer, and I believed that no one else had ever thought of it because I had never read it anywhere. This ground-breaking awareness—one that I was sure God gifted to me on a silver platter—was this: "Fear is the opposite of love." I knew that this would change the way people think. I thought it would change the world. I just needed to write it down and share it.

I spoke to some friends and shared this kernel of life-changing truth. Their response was surprising to me. They had heard something very similar, so they suggested that I read Marianne Williamson's book *A Return to Love*. "She talks about that, too," they said. It just so happened I had a trip planned and it's always good to read on a plane. I'll never forget that plane ride and that experience. As I read Williamson's book, the tears ran down my face. "This is it," I thought. "These are the exact truths that I had wanted to share." "This is MY book," I remember thinking. It made me feel horrible, I confess. Here I thought I had come upon a brand-new truth for humanity! And someone else got there first and wrote it down before I had a chance to do it. My craving to write was squelched in that moment. In that place on my timeline, my worldview was one of scarcity rather than abundance. Rather than embracing that I truly was onto something, I chose to feel minimized and irrelevant simply because it was already being written about by someone else.

A few years went by, and getting the urge to write, and again wanting to write a book that would unlock secrets for humankind, I wanted to point out the amazing and undeniable parallels between major religious thinking. As I looked around, it seemed like several major religious institutions had parallel concepts. Just like before, I shared my thoughts with friends, who then said that I should read Carolyn Myss's book *Anatomy of the Spirit*. I didn't cry that time. I was surprised and a little sad. I thought that I had made a super important discovery. Again. And again, I chose to feel small and defeated.

For decades, I allowed these experiences to act as a stop sign and a mute button. Instead of seeing them as encouragement, I allowed them to deflate my ego and zap my energy. Until now. The key word here is "ego," of course. I suffer from a kind of insecure-egomania. It has been difficult to balance these conflicting energies within me. And I am learning. Balance is a major key. The déjà vu phenomenon is real. I have come to appreciate that it is not a bad thing. Sure, many people have read Marianne Williamson's or Carolyn Myss's books. And then some people will read my musings and learn about how amazing those authors are and then go read their work—which has continued and evolved and both women are even more dynamic because they remain open to possibility.

My ego diminished my concept of what I could offer. It took a loving presence to remind me that libraries are full of books. There are shelves of books on the very same topic with dozens of different authors! In a very real way, this is another example of *both . . . and*. There is room for all those other books *and* for mine! There is only one "me." I am unique in my perception and the way in which I articulate an idea or concept is about me. It may provide an open door to another pilgrim on this journey called life. My profound desire is to share insight and share the light within me so that you may find the light within you. I know it's there.

For all these reasons and more, words matter. In the New Testament, I love the end of John's Gospel. He writes: "[T]here are also many other things that Jesus did; if every one of them were written down, I suppose that the world itself could not contain the books that would be written down." This is true for us as well. There is always more to say and more to ponder.

As you proceed in life, I encourage you to use your words wisely. Pay attention to your choice of vocabulary. Pay attention to the way others speak. Our choices reveal so much. Remember the powerful impact that our words have—power to create and power to destroy. This is why we need to listen to ourselves; we need to learn to choose words with intention; and we need to pay attention and speak with the compassion and the integrity of Ruiz's First Agreement: "Be impeccable with your word."

## PART II

# Wonder Matters:
# Pay Attention

*"Some people have a wonderful capacity to appreciate again and again, freshly and naively, the basic goods of life, with awe, pleasure, wonder, and even ecstasy."*

—Abraham H. Maslow

In the third *third* of my lifetime on this earth, I discovered the joy of wonder: *wonder* as a noun and *wonder* as a verb. I am a traveler. I know that I am on a journey. And probably like many of you, I am an observer. I see things. I wonder. I wonder a lot! I am fascinated by questions. I have so many questions! There is so much mystery in this lifetime. And there is so much wonder! I have greater peace of heart pondering and wondering.

How can we believe that we are correct or right on any one issue when issues are so incredibly complex? We can only articulate our experience to the best of our ability within the construct of our individual time and our personal place. Actually, that is what the writers of biblical scripture also did. Scripture was divinely inspired and divinely assembled into one place called the Bible. That is miraculous in and of itself! The love of God is inerrant, for sure. And any time we try to consolidate the infinite, there is room for error. It only makes sense that some things are timeless and others simply do not fit our context of time and place anymore.

Wonder, the noun, is expressed in awe and amazement. It surprises and reveals at the same time. We feel it quite often as children and then we get busy. We begin to take for granted the rotation of this whirling planet we live on. We forget. We forget how to wonder. We forget until something miraculous happens, as if cascading through space on a giant ball hurling around the sun at sixty-seven thousand miles per hour wasn't miraculous enough! Or until we simply pay attention. Pay attention to what surrounds us all the time and we just didn't notice or forgot to observe the sheer wonder of it all.

Wonder, the verb, plays an important role when our doubts invite us to ask really good questions. To wonder is to ponder thoughtfully, without attachment to right or wrong. Wonder invites us to be curious and adventurous. Wondering is like sailing or gliding—allowing the wind to take you. No accident there. I'll be talking about *wind* in upcoming chapters. In ancient Hebrew, the word for wind (*ruach*) is the same word as breath and Spirit. I wonder why that might be?

Barbara Brown Taylor says in her book *An Altar in the World*, "Earth is so thick with divine possibility that it is a wonder we can walk anywhere without cracking our shins on altars." Our spiritual shins must be black and blue for all the wonder that surrounds us. Our bodies are extraordinary and life is a miracle! The world around us is mysterious and awe-inspiring. In his essay entitled "The World As I See It," Albert Einstein wrote: "The most beautiful experience we can have is the mysterious . . . Whoever does not know it and can no longer wonder, no longer marvel, is as good as dead, and his eyes are dimmed." There is a passage in the Old Testament in the book of Ezekiel when the prophet looks out at a field of dry bones. God commands him: "Prophesy to the bones."[1] It's a great story, one that I explicate a little later in this book. A quick synopsis is this: There is a field full of dry, dry bones. These bones come alive again in the story. As dramatic as that sounds, the point here is that we are surrounded by things that can take our breath away when we merely stop and wonder about the treasure trove of life.

Wonder is wonderful, wonder-filled, and wondrous! All at the same time!

---

1    Ezekiel 37.

# CHAPTER 4

# Wonder of Color

When I was in my forties, one of my very best friends asked me why I always wore brown. I didn't know what she was talking about. I hadn't done it on purpose and I honestly didn't believe her and I tried to deny it. "Brown? Really?" "So," she said, "let's take a look at your closet." We went up to the walk-in closet I had. I watched as she rearranged my clothing by hue and shade. I was shocked at what I saw. Brown. Beige. Light brown. Dark brown. Gray. And more brown. One might try to spruce up the vocabulary a bit and say: russet, tan, coffee, or beige. The reality is that she was right. Nearly all my clothes were brown. Not a yellow, a red, a blue, or a magenta in sight!

Where did my color go? I didn't know the answer then. Perhaps I was too close to it. Perhaps I wasn't paying attention. In fact, I didn't realize that paying attention is a life skill, one that I've come to appreciate as I age. It took some very long periods of intentional discernment on my part. During a clergy retreat where the topic was creativity, the speaker talked about "creative wounds" that most of us walk around with. I knew exactly what she meant because the memory of my creative wound had emerged during my sabbatical the previous year. It happened when I was in eighth grade in an art class. I remember the project. I remember working on it. And I remember really liking what I had created. I can still see it. It was a pattern of repetitive parallel curving lines that I had painted bright colors in an alternating pattern that was quite pleasing to me. I thought it was really cool. And then I was aware of the art teacher standing behind me . . . not saying anything. And then he spoke. "You aren't hoping to take any art classes in high school . . . I hope . . . are you?" I felt sliced and diced . . . There it was. It was the biggest "your artwork stinks" that I could have ever been delivered. Color left me that day and I turned to brown—inside and out.

There I was: a grown woman looking into my closet as if for the first time. Seas of brown. I was surprised, I must admit, and not in a good way. It wasn't a conscious decision on my part. It was just what I wore.

I was brown on the outside because I was *brown* on the inside. I wasn't aware of the depth of passion within me. I was oblivious to the glorious shades of yellow, magenta, and purple! The wonder of color first articulated itself to me in clothing. I started wearing bright colors. To this day, bright tie-dye is my absolute favorite! I call it my "happy place." I just can't have enough tie-dye in my closet!

When I took a sabbatical during the pandemic of 2021, I took the time to notice color all around me. I noticed it most of all in nature. As a pastor, people will often say that they find God in nature on Sunday morning and that it is somehow better than a worship service indoors. In the early days of my ministry, I smiled politely and I didn't understand. I honestly did not believe them. It was not the same, I was sure! It could not be the same! Over the years, I've come to appreciate the wonder of God's creation so much that I finally have come to understand why people might say such a thing. Don't get me wrong. I still love a good worship service and a thought-provoking sermon and the fellowship of Sunday morning coffee hour. I just also understand the presence of the Divine in all those colors in nature!

Take green. We learn basic colors when we are young. It's when we get older and decide to paint the bathroom that we realize that there are dozens of shades of green! Translate that into the wonder of green in nature. That pine tree over there is green. Take a closer look. The pine needles on top are one shade of green and the pine needles on the bottom are another. Now look at the oak tree right next to it. Those leaves are green and they represent three more different shades of green. Green may be one vocabulary word and when we pay really close attention, we see a multitude of diverse colors.

Take blue. The blue ocean in the Bahamas is a different color than the blue ocean of Maine. The blue sky in Montana is not the same color as the blue sky in Hawaii. All the colors are like that. Colors are full of wonder and are wonderful, at the same time. It is a wonder and for me, it's one of those things that proves there's an energy at work that is divine. In fact, for me, it proves that the Divine loves diversity!

I'm not going to go through every color. I wonder if God isn't particularly fond of blue and green because these two are so prominent in Creation. But then again, I live in New England. In the hills outside Sedona, one wouldn't be able to say that! It's the same for all the other colors. Take a look for yourself. Slow down first. Breathe into them and look—really look.

Georgia O'Keeffe often talked about her method of enlarging what seemed small. She used color and size to accentuate what would otherwise go unnoticed. Look at the wonderful paintings that Georgia O'Keeffe realized. They are rich in size and color. They are extraordinary because she took the time to pay attention, to really look, and to enter into that world of natural wonder!

# CHAPTER 5

# Wonder of Sound

Music has always been an important part of my life. My father loved the big bands and he had the most amazing singing voice. I always loved to sing and my voice is a blending voice. I match other people's pitch or I harmonize easily with them. Just like color, I took music for granted. I've sung in choirs and choruses all my life. Playing an instrument was an unspoken requirement in my family of origin. Playing in a band or orchestra is especially fun because the sounds of the different individual instruments make such lovely sound together. I love this as a good metaphor for people being so different and having different gifts and when they work together, magic happens. It's a symphony!

Music is a human-made sound. I love that it is mathematical and infinite in its manifestations. I also love the music in nature. Around the time that I noticed the color green, I started listening to birds. So many different bird calls! It's a wonder! I have a friend, a birder, who goes out on her birthday every year with a group of friends in order to identify the number of birds by their call equal to the number of years she's been alive. She just turned fifty-nine and within a couple of hours last birthday, they had identified that many different birds by their songs.

As I write this, I hear the birds calling: gulls mostly, and there are some ducks and some land birds. I'm no birder and I'm sure there is a cardinal in that tree over there. I also hear the sound of the ocean as the waves crash on the rocks below. The tide is coming in so the sound has been changing over the last few minutes. The loud splashing on the rocks diminishes as the tide comes in. Over time there are fewer waves, and the splashes diminish so that soon it sounds more like wind in the trees until the water is as high as it is going to get. It's almost quiet now except for a gull or passing lobster boat. "Splash" becomes "swoosh." "Swoosh" then becomes "shhhh." And slowly the reverse happens. Shhhh becomes swoosh becomes splash. It's a wonder!

One of my favorite vocal coaches, Peggo Horstman Hoaes, taught me a delightful vocal exercise called toning. It is such a fun activity! It's possible to do alone and just let sound emerge through improvisation. It is also fun in a group. Someone leads with a sound or a tone and then, listening to an inner intuition, modulates that tone as the spirit suggests. Singing with another, one can choose to match, to harmonize, or to add percussive sounds accordingly. There's no wrong answer. It's all just natural sound. Sound coming from the soul. There were times during a lesson when we were toning for ten or fifteen minutes and had no concept of time passing. We were floating on the emerging frequencies. It can be so meditative and relaxing. Sound can be so soothing.

And sound can be so disturbing. If it weren't so, would sound effects be in a category all its own at the Oscars? I am so susceptible to sound in movies that I will mute the scary parts (if I watch them at all). During suspenseful movies, I'll hit mute because it can be way too much of a sensory overload for me.

There is a story in the Bible about finding YHWH [God] in the sheer silence.[1] It's a famous passage found

---

1   In the ancient Hebrew language, the name for God was never spoken and when written, there were no vowels (historically, written Hebrew did not include vowels). In modern times, you will see YHWH and you will see Yahweh.

in 1 Kings 19 as the Prophet Elijah was sent to meet up with YHWH. God was not in the thunder (that time). We expect that God would be in something so powerful and earth-shaking. God was not in the wind (that time). Wind and God are almost synonymous, so that was a surprise. God wasn't where anyone expected God to be. God was in the sheer silence. God is wherever God decides to be. It's a wonder that we keep trying to define God and build a little box to put God into. Will we never learn?

Sound accompanies us every day. It affects our mood. It can alter our disposition. Sound motivates. Sound provokes. Sound inspires. Sound is a wonder.

# CHAPTER 6

# Wonder of Rhythm

As human beings, we have an internal rhythm produced by beating hearts. Tha-dum. Tha-dum. Tha-dum. We aren't aware of the rhythm until it somehow changes and otherwise causes a problem. And it's always there. Always beating. Another wonder.

In her paper "Primal Patterns: Towards a Kinesthetic Hermeneutic," professor, worship designer, author, preacher and ritual artist Dr. Marcia McFee presents the wonder of rhythm and movement within each person. Having distilled the findings of several neuromuscular researchers, in her own workshops Dr. McFee now presents the idea that as creations of a divine and rhythmic Creator, we each have a particular rhythmic signature. We resonate or vibrate at one of four modes of energy, or "primal patterns." Some of us move with catalyzing rhythmic energy, one that invigorates and animates. Some of us have a more formalized and ordered rhythm that leads us to put order into any systems that appear to need shaping. Then, there is a playful energy that enjoys interaction with others and connecting on an interpersonal level. The fourth rhythmic energy is thoughtful and meditative, somewhat slow moving. Each person is unique and each person has a rhythm that feels like "home" to them.

We'll notice a ticking clock all of a sudden. It was ticking before we noticed it. And even once we have heard it, when we get busy it fades into the background again. The pulsing tick is always there. It fades in and out of our awareness. Without rhythm, where would dancers find their direction? How would they know whether to dance a foxtrot or a tango? Without conductors leading the band, how would instrumentalists know how long to hold a note?

It's a wonder!

Marching bands have always used rhythm to keep marchers in step. The drumline is the largest section of the band. There's nothing like a John Phillip Sousa march to get things going and keep the pulsing sound moving along!

The use of rhythm isn't a modern phenomenon. In human history, ancient ships powered by enslaved rowers used the steady beat of drums to keep the rowers' pace constant or to speed up or to slow down. In the biblical story of Jericho (Old Testament; book of Joshua, chapter 6) the Israelites walked around and around and around that city until the walls of Jericho came falling down. For six days, once a day Joshua's people marched around the city, blowing their trumpets. On the seventh day, they walked around seven times with trumpets blowing and then they shouted! All that sound and rhythm together was magnificent and destructive! No wonder the city walls fell! The noise must have been tremendous.

Sometimes quiet, sometimes thunderous, rhythm is a wonder and it is a very real, very crucial element to our humanity. Like a heartbeat. Like the tides of the ocean. Like the phases of the moon. The depth of our awareness fades in and out. Life's rhythm is present whether we notice it or not.

Wonder is truly a gift. We are full of wonder when we are children. Early in our lives, things are wonder-filled and wonderful. As we age, we learn to take things for granted. We become numb to wonder. It takes effort to snap out of it. Sometimes it takes a tragedy or major life event. It is possible to regain our sense of wonder. And when we do, we don't always pause our busy lives at the wonder of color, sound, and rhythm. We are struck by the wonder of cloud formations, sunsets, animals, and the list goes on and on and on. We are surrounded by wonder. What if we were to stop every once in a while and pay attention. "Behold!" the writers of the Bible say.[1] They want us to stop and to notice the Presence of the Divine and they are pointing to the everyday miracles and wonders that surround us all the time.

And while you are paying attention to the noun wonder, don't neglect the verb! Wondering is a sacred practice. Wonder about things. Put Google away and resist the urge to know every answer. Sit with the wondering. Sit with the ambiguity. Become comfortable with imagination. Wonder what something would look like or be like or sound like. There is divinity in wondering. Actually, there is divinity in all of the wonders and the wondering. Divinity is trying to get our attention. All the time. I wonder what our world would be like if more of us tuned into the divinity and wondered together a more beautiful human existence.

---

1    There are more than a thousand instances of "Behold!" in the Bible.

## PART III

# Spirituality Matters: Divinity Is All Around Us

*"This holy calling is not about having all the answers but leaning into the questions by which you might discover who God has called you to be—for the sake of the world. God loves us so much. Jesus doesn't ask us to get it right, but to be in relationship—with him and with others."*

—Karoline Lewis (*Belonging*, xiii)

Theism is the belief in the existence of a divine entity that is both energy and essence, which is responsible for all creation and interacts with humanity. I believe that Divinity accompanies us. Divinity guides us and there is Divinity within us that transforms a normal life into a spectacular life—a life resplendent with wonder and possibility. We are, after all, just muddy Buddhas. Everyone has a story, a gift and a message. Everyone has an inner light. I share my story to encourage you to share your story. The light within me is just one spark that burns within all of Creation. You have a spark, too. We all do.

In a world that has been deeply influenced by a system of religion that is grounded in the Judeo-Christian experience, the accepted word for the Divine is "God." And for many people, painful experiences that took place in a church have been attributed to "God." So much so, that the word God itself can cause pain. That pain is not of God. There is a difference between what humans have done "in the name of God" or Jesus or the Holy Ghost, and the creating Energy that many people call "God."

I love how the mythology of *Star Wars* found a word that described divinity without entering into any kind of debate: The Force. "May the Force be with you." It is that nameless energy that pulses through all living creatures. And yes, there is a dark side to that mythology. I stand with Yoda—holding fast that the force of good overpowers the force of the dark side.

"God" may be too charged a word for some folks because of difficult or painful situations in their past. So, they use another word. *Source*, perhaps. *Presence*, perhaps. Twelve-step recovery groups use *Higher Power*. What I know to be true is this: There is an insistent, persistent flow of "love energy" that attends to us across time and space. This divine Presence is consistent and at times pervasive. People of the Judeo-Christian tradition know Psalm 23 and they know the last line: "Surely goodness and mercy shall follow me all the days of my life." I believe in this.

A theology of a Divine Presence appears in nearly all tribes and human groups. It is felt by some and not others. Those who sense its presence try to articulate it. They paint pictures. They write poetry. They sing songs or make music. Myths emerge and religions attest to this Presence. I am comfortable continuing to use the word God because I know what I mean. Find your word and please understand where I'm coming from when I say "God."

Historically, once religions are established or developed, they then try to control the outcome or even the Presence of the Divine, itself. The Spirit, the Holy Spirit, that is, is like a wild goose alone—elegant and unpredictable. Religions codify, classify, and otherwise categorize human behavior and, just like Genesis 1, when the Almighty declared that "it was good," human beings decide what is acceptable or not according to the system they have created.

Here are a few examples. Genesis 1:28 says: "God blessed them, and God said to them, 'Be fruitful and multiply, and fill the earth and subdue it; and have dominion over the fish of the sea and over the birds of the air and over every living thing that moves upon the earth.'" Much later, when Moses had led the Israelites out of slavery in Egypt, they found themselves wandering and wondering about their future. Moses was summoned by God to go up the mountain called Mount Sinai, where they believed that God lived. When he came down, he had with him the Ten Commandments, etched on slates of stone. Rules have their place in society. As these early Israelites continued their journey, a legal system emerged within their society. Some laws, like the Ten Commandments, were out of devotion to God and some were necessary for survival. These Israelites were forced by circumstance into a nomadic lifestyle just trying to survive the brutality of their time. There were a number of laws about what to eat and what not to eat. There were laws about who to marry and how to take care of one another. In Deuteronomy 25:5, it says, "When brothers reside together, and one of them dies and has no son, the wife of the deceased shall not be married outside the family to a stranger. Her husband's brother shall go in to her, taking her in marriage, and performing the duty of a husband's brother to her." It was lawful and seen as merciful for the man to take his brother's wife as his own wife. They called it levirate marriage. I imagine that it was believed to be a compassionate law because in their culture women could not lawfully own anything. How, then, could a woman alone survive? Widows might have easily been doomed to a life of begging or prostitution without the levirate marriage laws. Many laws were established because these laws made sense to them and to their survival at the time. There were, in fact, 623 enforceable laws in the Old Testament.[1] That's 613 laws plus the original Ten Commandments.

Whatever did not make sense to them, whatever was simply not "the way we do things" was deemed unacceptable and was labeled an abomination. It simply was not what they felt they needed or wanted to do in order to survive. A wonderful example that challenges our modern understanding is the law about not eating lobster. To these ancient people, fish swam and animals walked. That was normal. That was the way things were. And God also created lobsters—fish that walk! A fish that walks is too strange to understand. Lobsters were therefore an abomination.

Another example is in their understanding of agriculture. They couldn't plant two different kinds of seed in the same field. That was an abomination to them. That wasn't the way they did things.

1   Jewish tradition teaches that there are 613 commandments, called *Mitzvot*; plus the Ten Commandments.

Another example is procreation. Since God ordered them to procreate, they did not take kindly to men who did not want to take women as wives or concubines in order to have children. It was believed that men carried life in their seed, and women were simply incubators. They had no modern understanding of biology. So, a man "lying with a man" was an abomination, which meant that this isn't the way we do things. Neither the word nor these actions were immoral in their society. It simply wasn't done.

Fast forward to our century and modern culture, the word "abomination" carries a moral value. In today's world, an abomination is something that causes disgust or hatred. This is vastly different from "that isn't something we do." One word means something in one century and may mean something vastly different two thousand years later. *Abomination* is one of those words.

LGBTQI+ people have paid heavy consequences for this misunderstanding. Not taking into consideration the historical-cultural context has been misleading at best and dangerous at worst. Church people thought they understood the meaning of the word abomination and made some really big errors in judgment. This one word has been used as a weapon against an entire group of people and many have suffered. Many of us have become aware of this mistake and many churches have tried to make amends. We now know better. And we're trying hard not to perpetuate the harm that has come from this misinformation.

It's important to note that I make a distinction between religion and spirituality. Religion is a system of faith practices. It is an institution with particular rules that govern it. Spirituality is the recognition that there is a divine power greater than humanity at work in the world. Religion decides and dictates. Spirituality ponders and wonders. Religion marches to a set rhythm. Spirituality flies one moment and crawls the next. Religion is predictable. Spirituality is anything but predictable! Religion is a box, with set parameters. Spirituality is more like a river, expressing itself in a variety of ways, flowing where it wills.

In our modern culture, where we have so many people who have been hurt by religion, we have become very creative about not sounding "too religious." Rather than say *God* or acknowledge any kind of Divinity about the moment, we use words like "coincidence" or "serendipity," "chance" or "prov- idence," "fate" or "destiny" or "karma." We go to great lengths to avoid sounding *religious*.

In his book *Synchronicity: An Acausal Connecting Principle*, psychologist Carl Jung used the word "syn- chronicity" to describe a "perceived meaningful coin- cidence." Synchronicity is when our perception points to meaning when we see meaning in the coincidence. We can ponder meaning and strive for meaning in the happenings of our lives. Working as a chaplain in a major trauma hospital, I learned to use the word "meaning" as a way to enter into spiritual dialogue with hospital patients and their families. This isn't a coincidence. It is a demonstration of my point. It has become difficult to talk about God's involvement in our lives because even the word *God* carries so many preconceived notions.

We do the best we can with the language that we have, all the while acknowledging that words often minimize rather than augment. When discussing the Divine, one might reach for the biggest word possible.

In these upcoming pages, I will use a Trinitarian God model to explore the love extended by a Creator, by a Redeemer, and by a Sustainer, as expressed in the Christian tradition. When I was a child, we sang, "Praise Father, Son and Holy Ghost." At some point the *ghost* became *spirit*. And somewhere along the line, the overbearing masculine nature of God was softened by the feminine images that, although they are hard to find, are very present in those pages of centuries-old scripture. Some progressive churches are not afraid to utter the words "Our Mother, our Father" when reciting the Lord's Prayer. And the irony is that Jesus prayed in the Aramaean language. The truest translation of the words he spoke were not "our father." What he said was closer to "Oh Birther, Father-Mother of the cosmos."

Remember how the Little Prince's friend, the fox, in the book by Antoine de Saint-Exupéry, says that "words are the source of misunderstanding." While this is certainly true, language—which is made up of words—is all we've got. And our paying attention to our word choices matters.

# CHAPTER 7

# Creative Love

Like many people who grew up in the Christian tradition, I was hurt by the institution when I realized that I was a same-gender-loving woman. This realization came as a result of getting sober and following the twelve-step program of Alcoholics Anonymous. It was 1994 and I was married to a man and had two daughters. At that time, I had been a member of a PCUSA (Presbyterian) church for fourteen years. I went to the minister for advice. He seemed to listen and his tone was kind—at first. Then he took a book off his shelf and handed it to me, "This book can help you get over this business." I saw that it was one of those "conversion" books that my LGBTQI+ friends had warned me about. And then he said plainly, "If you can be normal again, you'd be welcome to stay." There it was. This religious leader did not consider me "normal."

I was in a faith-based, twelve-step therapy group at that time. There were seven of us and a facilitator. When I came out in that group, one of the women stood up and yelled at me: "God did not get you sober so that you could screw women and destroy your family!" I was horrified and felt ashamed. It wasn't even about sex for me. The group made it sexual and shameful. They sent me to Sexaholics Anonymous. After three of those meetings, I knew that I was on the wrong path and my awakening identity was not about an addiction.

I was devastated. My minister did not think I was normal and the therapy group thought that I was destroying my family. I became despondent and depressed. I did not want to destroy my family. "They would be better off without me," I thought. Those dangerous words led me to make a decision. I called my children on the phone so that I could hear their sweet voices one last time. I then called my best friend to thank her for being my best friend. She heard something in my voice and said, "I need you to come to my house. Right now. If you aren't here in fifteen minutes, I'll never forgive you. Bye!" She hung up. I had no choice.

Once at her house, she inquired, "You go to those AA meetings every day, what do they say to do?" "Oh, it's stupid," I said. "They say to go to a meeting." "OK, let's go." She called the AA information hotline to find the next meeting, and then she took me there. There was a large table in the center of the room and people sitting around it. There were also people sitting all along the wall, too. My friend and I sat together along the outside wall. I was feeling hopeless and angry. I didn't ask for this! The life I knew had taken a major turn in a direction that confused and terrified me. This whole gay thing wasn't my idea! As I sat there, I could feel myself getting more and more agitated. I wasn't listening to the speaker. I just wanted the pain to stop. And then the speaker called on me. I'll never forget: "You, in the back," pointing directly at me. "Tell us what's going on."

For the next several minutes, I talked. Well, honestly, I spewed! I let it all out. All the anger, the sadness, the surprise, the worry. And then, the most incredible thing happened. The appearance of the room, which had people sitting all around the table in the middle and people sitting all around the outside, began to change. Two circles of human souls—all looking at me. As I dug deep into my despair and emptied my sorrow, an incandescent glow appeared, growing stronger by the second, and shone on each person's face. The radiance grew. It was like one of those paintings from the Middle Ages where the people had these amazing halos shining around their heads. That's not all. A thin string of light appeared—a string of light from each person's heart to mine—connecting me to them and all of them to each other. A web of light. A luminous web. A safety net. I saw the light and I felt powerful love. I had never before felt such love. The message I received was undeniable. I was loved. I was loved beyond my imagination. And I was perfect just the way God created me. It took my breath away. The image of that room that night is indelibly engraved in my mind's eye. In church talk, we call this a "mountaintop experience," one that has never left me. From that night on, I never doubted God's love for me. Not for one minute, no matter what any person in any church or any institution might say.

When the meeting concluded, people surrounded me with care and concern. I learned that the therapy group was funded by a local Catholic church that was incredibly homophobic. I was not the only LGBTQI+ person who had been hurt by religion.

It took me a lifetime of experience and Spirit's persistence to get where I am today. "Where exactly are you today?" you may ask. I'm sure you've heard of the "separation of church and state." I have come to believe that there is also a separation between *church* and *God*, and between *institution* and *Spirit*. I see the Divine all around and I believe that there is a foundational difference between *God* and *church*. Yes, the church hurt me and maybe the church hurt you, too. God didn't. God couldn't. God is love. Any and all limitations, judgments and concepts of scarcity—or anything less than love—that can be found in sacred scripture were inspired by the fear that humans experience rather than a Divinity that is always and only love. And yes, I found an expression of Christianity that allows me the space to explore the Divine beyond the boundaries of any one denomination. I found a Christian denomination that allows for a variety of paths to God. I am beyond grateful.

When I was a child, we all ate dinner together: my mother, father, brother, sister, and me. It was already out of character for me to be bold. One night everything changed. I boldly announced at the dinner table:

"When I grow up, I'm going to work for God!" My family laughed at me in a way that hurt me to the core. When I was hurt by others, my habit was to retreat into myself. So, I never spoke another word about it. Many years later, God was leading me toward a seminary education and I remembered that announcement. It became part of my Call story. All ministers have them. For me, having left that Presbyterian church, I was led to a very charismatic Catholic church that welcomed people from recovery. They served grape juice at the Eucharist, which is unheard of. They also welcomed LGBTQI+ persons with open arms. The priest blessed gay unions in the days before Marriage Equality.[1] This wasn't a church that "hated the sin and loved the sinner," which is another hurtful behavior of many churches. This church loved ALL God's children. And this church believed that women shared a call to be priests. The assistant pastor to the lead priest was a woman by the name of Mary. Like I said, not a typical Catholic church! They still exist to this day,

1    Marriage Equality: prior to 2015 it was not legal nationally for people of the same gender to legally marry. The U.S. Supreme Court ruled that year that marriage was not confined to couples of opposite genders.

having been excommunicated by the Roman Catholic Church and joining up with the American Catholic Church. During Mass one day, Mary was preaching on the Matthew passage "You are the light of the world."[2] I heard—or felt—a voice saying, "She's talking to you, you know." It was profound and uncanny—and I did know. Women weren't ministers when I was much younger. When I was little and said that I would work for God, I figured that I would become a nun. That is, until I found out that nuns are Catholic and I wasn't Catholic. Oh, and they don't get married and don't have children, which I had and I did.

For many years, I considered that innocent declaration as prophetic. I was on a path to "work for God," having achieved a Masters of Divinity Degree and a Doctorate of Ministry in Preaching and serving as a local church pastor for nearly twenty years. Only recently have I realized something else about

---

2    Matthew 5:14–16: "You are the light of the world. A city built on a hill cannot be hidden. No one after lighting a lamp puts it under the bushel basket, but on the lampstand, and it gives light to all in the house. In the same way, let your light shine before others, so that they may see your good works and give glory to your Father in heaven."

that prophecy. For all these years, I have actually been working for the Christian institution called *church*. I realized that *church* is one thing and God is quite another. This book is a step toward me truly working for God, in the largest sense of the word. God doesn't belong to a church or a religion. God is much bigger than the attempts we can make. Without any disrespect to those attempts (unless they hurt people—and some do), I am now on a much wider path. Where it may lead, only God knows.

Since I like puns I might say that whereas my background is *fundamentally* Christian, do not confuse me with *fundamental* Christianity. The word "fundamental" means "underlying" or "foundational." I was raised Christian. I have belonged to several of the Protestant expressions, as well as Catholicism. And there is an expression of Christianity that refers to itself as fundamental or fundamentalist. This group of Christians holds to a belief that the Bible is always to be taken literally and that it is inerrant, that is, incapable of ever being wrong. These fundamental Christians reject ideas of gender fluidity or the idea that God is ever female in her expression. In fact, they perceive that their expression of Christianity is the only one that is right, true, and correct.

Perhaps my pun makes more sense now. Fundamentalists would never want me. In their worldview, I am a heretic. There are plenty of reasons. To name a few: I am a same-gender loving woman and I love the mothering images of God in the Bible. More importantly, they wouldn't want me because I know I'm "not right." I believe that the answer is in the question and not the other way around. I have belonged to churches that had "the" answer. They believed that they were "right." Wanting to be part of their church meant that none of my previous baptisms were good enough, for example. I was, for these reasons, baptized at least four different times as an adult. I never lasted very long in those churches though, because I wasn't ever comfortable thinking that I had "the" answer. "One size fits all" is not my theology. I've never been comfortable thinking that I was right when it comes to God. How can any human formula, which is by nature finite, define something that is by nature infinite? So, I ponder.

The first member of the Trinity is the Creator. Creation is the supreme act of love. It's as simple as that.

WORDS, WONDER, AND THE DIVINE IN YOU

Genesis 1 is all about Creation and it is about giving birth to a new way of life which was to be humanity's story and existence on this planet. God created by speaking. God spoke to create and God spoke calling what was created "good." The heavens, the earth, the sun, moon, stars, the land, the seas, the beasts of the air, the beasts of the sea, the creepy, crawling things on land. "Good." All of it good. All of it an act of love (Genesis 1).

In Genesis, chapter 2, we see that after God created a man, God instructed the man to name things. In the biblical tradition, naming is a demonstration of power. And to distinguish God's self from all other things, God defied being named. At first. The humans, the Israelites, insisted that God be called something. God conceded and it was a word not to be spoken aloud: YHWH. YHWH defied naming, defied definition, and could not be reduced to a spoken word, until humanity did it anyway.

In an effort to remain undefinable, unbridled, and pure life force, YHWH resisted. Moses pushed and pushed until finally YHWH gave in, saying: "Call me 'I AM.'" And there you have it. God is pure presence.

YHWH is pure creative presence. Pure creative presence is recognized by love, by acts of love. The wonder of nature. Love. The glory of the heavens, the sun, the moon, the sky. Love.

Generation after generation have dwelled upon the earth. Stories were told. Poetry was written. In the book of Deuteronomy, chapter 5, the Ten Commandments were given. Four are about loving God. Six are about loving your neighbor. Then in Deuteronomy, chapter 6, God instructed, "Love the LORD your God with all your heart, and with all your soul, and with all your might." Leviticus, chapter 19, adds: "Love your neighbor as yourself." YHWH is love and so love God, love your neighbor, love yourself.

There is a powerful word in ancient Hebrew: "hesed." "Hesed" is so divine in nature that it almost defies definition. It's God's enduring steadfast love. It is not the emotion of love. It's more than emotion. It's God's unbridled, all-encompassing, steadfast caring, which is God's behavior. Hesed is God's nature. "God's steadfast love endures forever" in Psalm 136. Hesed? Yes, hesed is timeless. From generation to generation we are exhorted to love God, love our neighbor and love ourselves. God's hesed will "pursue us all the days of our lives" (Psalm 23). Many translations use the word "follow." A more accurate rendering of the original word is "pursue." Sit with that for a moment. God's unquestionable love *pursues* you all the days of your life. A friend of mine says, "The Universe is benevolent by definition." That one belief can change how you view the world.

Three simple modes of behavior were cornerstone to the greatest commandment: love God, love your neighbor, love yourself. Sprinkled throughout the Old Testament stories of the faith ancestors are directives on good behavior above and beyond the sheer emotion of love. Life is not without its moments of questioning and fear, and then insecurity and judgment. So, the Israelites started adding laws. Their laws were meaningful for their context and were not meant to be timeless. Leviticus 11:9–12 warns against eating lobster. Things that crawl belong on land, and things that live in the sea will swim. This is what they believed to be normal. This thinking made the eating of lobster an abomination. Leviticus 19:19 prohibits planting wheat and corn in the same field. Whatever you do, don't touch a pig! The explanation is found in Leviticus 11:27. If we had continued with that one, we never would have had the NFL and the Super Bowl! The list goes on and on. For God's sake, don't get caught up in all 623 laws of the Old Testament, or you'll be selling your daughter into servitude as explained in Exodus 21. I'm not making this up![3]

The reality of the love of God can come to us in the "still, small voice," the way it did for Elijah in 1 Kings 19. The message is real. That *still, small voice* WILL overcome the doubts in this lifetime. That still, small voice WILL get our attention when we least expect it. Deep down we possess a *knowing* of the reality of God's love. The Old Testament prophet Jeremiah sings a mighty song of God's faithfulness to God's people in chapter 31, recounting all the times

---

3  Exodus 21:7–11: "When a man sells his daughter as a slave, she shall not go out as the male slaves do. If she does not please her master, who designated her for himself, then he shall let her be redeemed; he shall have no right to sell her to a foreign people, since he has dealt unfairly with her. If he designates her for his son, he shall deal with her as with a daughter. If he takes another wife to himself, he shall not diminish the food, clothing, or marital rights of the first wife. And if he does not do these three things for her, she shall go out without debt, without payment of money."

when God's people were guided out of bondage and led to better places. And then in verse 33, he says: "But this is the covenant that I will make with the house of Israel after those days, says the Lord: I will put my law within them, and I will write it on their hearts; and I will be their God, and they shall be my people." Divine Love is written on our hearts says Jeremiah.

I've heard it said that there are no atheists in a foxhole. I've not been in a foxhole and I understand this expression. I've seen it time and time again. People under stress have a profound yearning for a higher power, for their version of the luminous web that I experienced that night when I believed all was lost and met God instead. Based on my experience, I believe that it is because we are spiritual beings at our core. We are experiencing a physical life right now. And every once in a while, during this physical existence, we come to a "thin place": a place where the physical and the spiritual overlap in the most mysterious and life-giving manner.

# CHAPTER 8

# Redemptive Love

The second member of the Christian Trinity is Jesus, the Incarnated One. The institution of Christianity argued for centuries about the divine nature of Jesus. Was Jesus fully human and partially divine? Was Jesus partially human and fully divine? Clearly, based on history, they agreed that there was something powerfully *divine* about Jesus. Was he made up of "similar" substance as Divinity itself? Or was he made up of the "same" substance as Divinity? In the ancient Greek language, the difference between the words for *similar* and *same* is one letter. It's the letter "i" called "iota" in Greek. Here are two words: *homoousios* and *homoiousios*. There is an "i" in the second word. The first word means: "of the same substance." The second word, the one with the "i", means: "of similar substance." Have you ever heard the expression "not one iota"? This is how that expression came into being and how centuries of arguing led the institutional church, which was the Catholic Church, to the decision of "same substance." Once the church decided that Jesus was fully human and fully divine, the theological concept of the "Trinity," that is, a triune God, came into being. One in three.

Jesus is the "Word who became flesh." The writer of the Gospel according to John explains that the Word "was" at the beginning. With the most poetic and beautiful rendering, we read in the first chapter of John how God in the form of the Son of Man, later named Jesus, was present at Creation and made the conscious decision to live a life of a human being, thereby entering into our finite existence and limited physical form in order to model and exemplify redemption at its highest capacity.

What do I mean by redemption and why might it be necessary? We are spiritual beings having a corporal experience. During this physical manifestation, we are limited. There are boundaries and limitations to our experience. By default, we sometimes need to be liberated from those confines. That freedom is sometimes called salvation, sometimes redemption. Jesus extended grace to everyone. The thing about grace is that it isn't earned. Redemption happens when a spiritual being in its physical expression extends grace that exceeds human comprehension.

Biblical scholars talk about Incarnation with a capital "I." That's a neon sign that we need to pay attention to this word! Jesus, as a person who is fully divine, acted in the world and interacted with human beings.

At the end of Jesus' human life, he explained that followers of his "way" (a.k.a. love) would be imbued with the same Spirit that he possessed; that these followers would do even greater acts of compassion than he did. And in the meantime, he spent three years living a life of *hesed* and abundant grace. "From [God's] fullness we have all received, grace upon grace" (John 1:16). This is the message that is worthy of a bumper sticker. This is the message of God's *hesed*—not just the feeling called love. It is the behavior of abundant love. We have ALL received it. So much grace that saying it one time isn't enough. One time doesn't do it justice. It's more grace than you or I can imagine. God's abundance poured out for God's children/God's creation consistently, repeatedly for a three-year ministry in hopes that we would "get it";

that we would finally understand the depth of love that God has for each one of us. And some days we do. Many days, however, we still feel unloved or unworthy of love. The messages of the world that reduce us can be so prevalent and so loud. They drown out the message of the love of God. Fear takes over and we no longer hear God's still small voice.

Spending time with the Gospel of John extends to us the belief that it was the *life* of Jesus which calls us to a life of faith. So many people will emphasize the death of Jesus. They have bumper stickers with John 3:16 written out: "For God so loved the world that he gave his only begotten Son." I chafe when I hear a sacrificial lamb imagery. I won't deny that it meant something to the ancient Israelites. And for me, in my here and now, the fact that Jesus lived and loved and modeled God's *hesed*—that is *my* bumper sticker! Grace upon grace. Hesed Incarnate!

# CHAPTER 9

# Sustaining Love

Some Christians may explain that the Old Testament is where God the Father is found; the New Testament is where God the Son is found; and the Holy Spirit, given to us as demonstrated by the tongues of fire at Pentecost in the book of Acts in the New Testament, is with us now. Trinitarian theology holds that there are the three aspects of God: the Father, the Son, and the Holy Ghost. YHWH is the God of the Israelites who is one aspect of God, God the Creator. Jesus is God the Son, another equal and different aspect of God. Jesus did not leave us orphaned; he left to us the gift of the Holy Spirit, who claims that third aspect of God. Many churches will explain the Trinity to their children with the following example. There is water. When it freezes, it is ice. When it gets hot, it becomes steam. All three remain the same chemical compound of $H_2O$. God is much more fluid, keeping that water analogy, than a limited portrayal—and much more expansive.

To some extent, it might be reassuring to have three well-defined and very independent aspects of God that we can put neatly into three separate columns on a page or into three separate boxes neatly tied up with a bow. The reassurance might be short-lived when reality starts blurring the lines. This is one of those times when I question who created whom? I choose to believe in a God that is so dynamic that the mystery remains and the exact nature of this divine presence is at least somewhat unknowable.

Here is what I see. Triune theology is like a tapestry where threads of God the Father weave throughout both New and Old Testaments, and threads of the Incarnate Son, as demonstrated by that powerful redemptive love, weave throughout both Testaments, and yes, the threads that are Holy Spirit weave throughout both New and Old as well. Remember that a traditional perspective presents the Creator/Father dominating the Old Testament and the Incarnate/Son dominating the New Testament. Add to those two images the third member of the Triune God model, the Holy Spirit, who was promised by Jesus and who makes a huge entrance once Jesus is gone.

I want to offer some examples that blur that traditional approach, hoping to shed light rather than confuse. *Ruach*, the word for breath in ancient Hebrew, the language of the Old Testament, is also the word for Spirit. The breath of God is the Spirit of God. The Old Testament is full of images of the Holy Spirit, described as God's breath. The breath of God breathed life into the first human being in Genesis 1:7: "Then the Lord God formed man from the dust of the ground, and breathed into his nostrils the breath of life; and the man became a living being."

In Exodus 14:21, Moses led the Israelites away from Pharaoh's clutches and the divine wind of God parted the Red Sea. "Then Moses stretched out his hand over the sea. The Lord drove the sea back by a strong east wind all night, and turned the sea into dry land; and the waters were divided."

We also see evidence of the Holy Spirit in the book of Ezekiel, chapter 37:

[1] The hand of the Lord came upon me, and he brought me out by the spirit of the Lord and set me down in the middle of a valley; it was full of bones.

<sup>2</sup> He led me all round them; there were very many lying in the valley, and they were very dry.

<sup>3</sup> He said to me, "Mortal, can these bones live?" I answered, "O Lord God, you know."

<sup>4</sup> Then he said to me, "Prophesy to these bones, and say to them: O dry bones, hear the word of the Lord.

<sup>5</sup> "Thus says the Lord God to these bones: I will cause breath to enter you, and you shall live.

<sup>6</sup> "I will lay sinews on you, and will cause flesh to come upon you, and cover you with skin, and put breath in you, and you shall live; and you shall know that I am the Lord."

<sup>7</sup> So I prophesied as I had been commanded; and as I prophesied, suddenly there was a noise, a rattling, and the bones came together, bone to its bone.

<sup>8</sup> I looked, and there were sinews on them, and flesh had come upon them, and skin had covered them; but there was no breath in them.

<sup>9</sup> Then he said to me, "Prophesy to the breath, prophesy, mortal, and say to the breath: Thus says the Lord God: Come from the four winds, O breath, and breathe upon these slain, that they may live."

[10] I prophesied as he commanded me, and the breath came into them, and they lived, and stood on their feet, a vast multitude.

Another example of Spirit Presence is found in John 1:1: "In the beginning was the Word and the Word was with God and the Word was God." This is a double metaphor linking Jesus to Genesis. Jesus is the embodiment of redemption or Salvation Incarnate. When we consider the Old Testament stories, redemption often holds center stage. Consider the story of Jonah who tried to escape God's task and was swallowed by a big fish only to end up where he, himself, needed to be anyway. There is redemption in the story of Noah and his family who are saved when Noah obeys God's command to build an ark. There is the story of Ruth[1] and the story of David,[2] to name a few. The Spirit of redemption and God's holy *hesed*

---

1  Ruth followed her mother-in-law Naomi back to her people, the Israelites, where she was taken in and became one of them by marrying Boaz, a descendant of Abraham and an ancestor to David and to Jesus.

2  David sinned against God and he repented and sought forgiveness.

surely pursues (see Psalm 23) our faith ancestors just as it promises to pursue us.[3]

Jesus made us a promise: "I will not leave you orphaned."[4] The promise of the Holy Spirit is undeniable. The reality of the Holy Spirit permeates the majority of the New Testament. Jesus defined this Spirit of truth: counselor, advocate, helpmate. The "paraclete" (Greek word used in the Gospel of John to express the third person in the Trinity) was who Jesus promised his followers. This Spirit would be the Helper, the Protector, the One who would accompany them and accompanies us always and in all ways. Modern New Age practitioners talk about energy, resonance, or vibration. Could these also be manifestations of this same Divine Presence we keep hoping to name?

While some Christian denominations embrace the mystery of the Spirit and often call themselves "Pentecostal," many Christians have resisted the power

3 The original word in the 6th verse of Psalm 23 is mistranslated with the word "follow." In truth goodness and mercy "pursue" us. They don't merely follow us.

4 Gospel of John 14:18.

of the Holy Spirit. They have decided to relegate that Spirit to a few particular biblical passages that are by nature located within historic events rather than here-and-now experiences. This reductionist mindset can be witnessed in the formal schedule of scripture readings for the church year. The institutional church devised a specific schedule and formalized the reading of scripture to particular times of the year. A "church calendar" was created and the Revised Common Lectionary, known as the RCL, was born. It was decided to use a three-year cycle, based on the Gospels of Matthew, Mark, and Luke. These three follow a similar pattern, sharing some of the same stories, and are known as the Synoptic Gospels, because they can be seen (optic) together (syn-) as one overarching story. The Gospel of John does not follow the same pattern. Precious stories (Greek word *pericope*) from John would be used now and again throughout the RCL.

This church calendar and the RCL follow a system of liturgical or church seasons in our churches. There are, for example, four weeks of anticipation or waiting for the baby to appear in the manger. This is known as Advent. There are then six weeks of preparation, a time called Lent, to face the bloody burdened cross and then rejoice at the redemptive empty tomb. Fifty days after the episode of the empty tomb, the church takes one day to read that magnificent appearance of the Holy Spirit at Pentecost in Jerusalem (The Book of Acts, Chapter 2). On that appointed day, otherwise reserved and stoic Christians will sing and clap and be amazed at the wonder of the magnificently blowing wind and the tongues of fire. The following Sunday, we settle back into our calm and controlled worship and our peaceful and measured lives. The third member of the Holy Trinity, the Holy Spirit, is relegated to one day. I do realize that there is small print in the RCL that refers to everything between the day of Pentecost and Advent as "the Season of Pentecost." I just haven't seen the Holy Spirit in all of its unpredictable, mysterious, and surprising glory being lived in the church communities where I have served. The system seems resistant to carrying that much mystery for that many weeks.

I recently discovered a community that likens the Holy Spirit to a Wild Goose. "A wild goose?" I thought. Imagining that this group had invented the metaphor, I soon learned that in actuality the ancient Celts were the ones who decided that a wild goose, when they are not in majestic flying formation, is awkward and gangly. When one of these flying creatures is on the ground interacting with human beings, it is rambunctious and unpredictable. The Celts believed that this was a much more fitting image than the gentleness and predictability of a New Testament dove. Christians in the sixth century pointed out that geese on the ground will protest vigorously and protect themselves and their loved ones ferociously. In modern times, social-justice-motivated Christians relate much more to the behavior of the wild goose than the docile dove. They show up at state houses to protest potential legislative injustices. They show up at Planned Parenthood to walk women seeking medical treatment safely to the door. A wild goose Christian doesn't sit back calmly and watch things happen. The Spirit of God will make itself known—loudly and proudly. Jesus foretold it and time has proven it.

Which one of these suits you? Does the tamed dove-like Spirit of God conform to your faith journey? Or do you relate more to an erratic, squawking goose-like Spirit of God that blows where it will and shows up at the most synchronistic moments? Be aware that your answer may indicate that you are creating God in your own image as opposed to the other way around. Surprises make many of us uncomfortable. We prefer predictability to providential mystery. That doesn't relate to our God. That relates to our fear. And if I am to listen to what I am putting into the world through this book, am I creating God in an image that I relate to? And then maybe it's a both . . . and.

There are at least 365 scriptural references to the Divine encouraging human beings not to be afraid. And even though we are reminded—sometimes gently, sometimes not so gently—we do fear. We fear and then we base our beliefs in fear rather than faith. Is there hope for us since we so predictably need to be reminded? The answer is "of course!" which leads me back to the raison d'être for this book. Let's pay attention to the decisions we make that are steeped in fear. Let's listen to the words that we choose that are based in inadequacy or lack. So much beauty and wonder and glory is right under our nose. All. The. Time.

# So, Here's the Thing

Fear serves a purpose in this fragile life we live. It informs us. It instructs us to run in the face of danger. It gives us the strength we need to push through menacing situations. Fear is useful. Until it's not. Until it doesn't serve us anymore. Fear can hold us back. It can cause us to lose opportunities. It can spawn misunderstanding and resentment and more. And perhaps the worst scenario is that it can separate us from the Divine.

The opposite of fear is love. Think about it. People believe that the opposite of love is hate. Actually, it's not. Hate is not the absence of love. Hate is the presence of fear made manifest. A friend shared with me her father's explanation of hate. When she and her sister were small, her sister didn't want to eat the mashed potatoes on her plate. She pushed the plate away and said, "I hate mashed potatoes." Their father said: "Are you afraid of your mashed potatoes?" Of course, they just looked at each other not at all understanding what he meant. Their father explained: "Hate is just fear. I don't think you are afraid of those poor mashed potatoes. So, you don't hate them, either." This lesson stuck with her and it gave me something to think about.

Many negative feelings can be peeled away to reveal fear underneath. Resentment is based in fear. Jealousy comes out of fear. And whenever you feel resentment and jealousy, you are actually feeling an absence of love. Marianne Williamson's work to demystify "*The Course in Miracles*" is an extensive deep dive in this area of thought. *A Course in Miracles* (also referred to as ACIM or the Course) is a 1976 book by Helen Schucman. The underlying premise is that the greatest "miracle" is the act of simply gaining a full "awareness of love's presence" in a person's life. Schucman said that the book had been dictated to her, word for word, via a process of "inner dictation" from Jesus. In 1992, Marianne Williamson appeared on *The Oprah Winfrey Show* and discussed the book. She has been presenting this material ever since.

I didn't understand this concept that love's opposite was fear—at least at first. I resisted it with determination. In the end, I realized that the passionate effort I was expending to disprove this fundamental principle was, in fact, based in fear. Fear that I was not as loving as I believed myself to be. And then, something else occurred to me—thanks to the Spirit's guidance, of course. This reality that fear is the opposite of love is not quantitative. It cannot be measured or calculated. And we don't have to judge it. We simply need to recognize it and work to develop that recognition sooner. The Divine wants the best for us and wants us to fulfill our potential as best we can. There are not tricks or traps. There are no gotchas.

Spirituality matters. Are we physical beings having a spiritual experience or are we spiritual beings having a physical experience? This is a great question and it's a question whose response can vary depending on the day and our frame of mind. Many might say the former—and that from time to time something of Divinity ekes into our physical lives. We were born, we live and we die. And there are many—this writer included—who give mystery a much higher role in the formula. Spirituality is all around us because Spirit dwells within us.

In my context, we talk about God-incidences because we don't believe in coincidences, because we believe that Divinity by whatever name intervenes often. God-winks are normal. They happen every day. We don't use those culturally accepted terms like *serendipity* or *luck*. We call out God-incidents and blessings. We are lucky that way.

I truly believe that we are spiritual beings first. We were Spirit before we became indwellers of these physical bodies and we will go back to being Spirit when the time comes. And isn't that what Jesus did? "Earth to earth, dust to dust."[1] And that is only part of our story. We ought to add: "spirit to Spirit."

I share my experience and my hope because I want to encourage you to share yours. I want to hear yours. My experience is my own and I pray that you will pay attention to your own experience as a result of me sharing mine. I am not trying to convert anyone. I do not believe that I'm right. I am not trying to push my

---

1 The exact phrase comes from the Church of England's *Book of Common Prayer* and is used for burial services. It is used today by many Christian denominations because it refers back to Genesis 1, when God formed the first human out of dirt, a.k.a. dust.

beliefs on anyone. I have learned to find beauty in the images of Christian scripture and translate accordingly. Just as I have learned to find beauty and truth in the images and metaphors of faith traditions outside Christianity. I pray that some might find a blessing in the process of my sharing.

Think back to the story of that golden Buddha covered with layers of mud and clay and broken glass. For centuries, no one knew what was truly underneath. We have an amazing treasure within us. We are covered with self-doubt and negativity—sometimes inflicted by others and sometimes self-inflicted. The result is the same: the *gold* within us is hidden from view. Here's the thing: we were created with that inner treasure and it is our life's work to uncover it.

May my ponderings encourage you in yours and may the wonder of this life fill all of us with joy—which is our call and our destiny.

# Acknowledgements

I am so grateful to everyone who helped this book come into being. I need to thank Pamela, Margie, and Amy, who were my initial "believing mirrors" and who walked with me before words appeared on the page. I want to thank all of my readers. Those brave souls who read the very first draft: Emily, Pamela, Peggo, and Arron. You were all so very encouraging and your "say more" comments helped me to practically double the book in size. Then come the second version readers: Thank you to Trudie, who is the most thorough proofreader I could have ever found. You taught me so much. Thank you to Kathy, John, Ruth, and Eszter— your comments were so helpful, so incredibly valuable, so affirming. And then God bless Pamela—who agreed to read it all again—and still she encouraged me to do more.

Thank you to the people who suggested how to get the final book published. So many options are available these days.

Thank you to everyone at First Parish Congregational Church, UCC, in East Derry, NH. The words left my head and the pages took form during the summer of 2022, when you granted me Study Leave—just to write.

Thank you to my beloved wife, Liz, who stands with me through thick and thin, ups and downs, good days and bad days. You are divine. I've known it since the day we met. And I am so very grateful that you are my partner in life.

# About the Author

Deborah Roof is an enthusiastic life-long learner and a passionate teacher. She is an ordained minister in the United Church of Christ with a Master of Divinity degree from Colgate Rochester Crozer Divinity School and a Doctor of Ministry in Preaching from the Chicago Theological Seminary. Deborah is fluent in French, holds a Master's degree in French Literature, and taught French for over twenty years. Intrigued by ancient archetypal wisdom, Deborah studied and became a Certified Veriditas Labyrinth Facilitator. Deborah and her wife, Liz, have four adult daughters, their daughters' four spouses, and four grandchildren.

# Advance Praise for
## *Words, Wonder, and the Divine in You*

"With humor and heart-filled honesty, Roof takes you on a journey of discovery back to yourself and your divinely inspired story. The words of this beautiful book will instill wonder in your soul, ignite your spirit, and bring love to the center of your life."

—Rev. Karoline M. Lewis, PhD, (ELCA); Author, Biblical Scholar, Professor of Biblical Preaching at Luther Seminary; Program Director, Festival of Homiletics

"Reading this book is like sitting down with a good friend over a cup of coffee, and talking about things that matter. Deborah Roof has opened her wise pastoral heart to us in this engaging work, inviting us to reimagine our lives, and the church, as wondrous expressions of divine love—where God is still and always speaking!"

—Rev. Anna Carter Florence, PhD, (PCUSA); Author, Biblical Scholar, Professor of Preaching at Columbia Theological Seminary

"Deborah Roof has a mystical experience in an AA meeting soon after coming out as queer. She later lets God nudge her to trade in her closet of brown garb for a wardrobe splashy with tie-dye. And even though she is a pastor, she doesn't try to sell us on the merits of church, but tells the truth that we can just as reliably–and more palpably–encounter the Divine outside of institutions.

At every turn, she reminds us that it's easy to encounter the sacred, because God-by-whatever-name-you-know-God has already been chasing after us with a love that will not let us go, nor let us talk ourselves down (or anyone else for that matter).

This little book of wonders is written in a warm, nourishing and approachable style rife with real life stories. It is a gift for anyone who has been burned by toxic Christian theology or just needs their longtime faith exfoliated to get at the tender fresh skin underneath."

—Rev. Molly Baskette, United Church of Christ Pastor and Author of *How to Begin When Your World is Ending: a Spiritual Field Guide to Joy Despite Everything*

"There is a heart beating in Deborah Roof's new book, "Words, Wonder and the Divine in You." In the chapter "Creative Love," she tells a story of trust given and rejected, followed by the healing miracle of a friend and a randomly chosen meeting that enveloped her in radical and holy inclusion. Roof's generosity with her own life invites readers to discover a spiritual core in their own experiences."

— Rev. Maren C. Tirabassi, United Church of Christ Pastor, Author of faith-based non-fiction, poetry and fiction

"So often, books about Christian spirituality that include theological reflection feel to the reader like memoirs. I love memoirs, but they don't give me new tools for making spiritual sense of life. Deborah Roof's *Words, Wonder, and the Divine in You* presents an original framework for introspection on the daily life of faith."

—Rev. Sarah Drummond, PhD; United Church of Christ Pastor and founding Dean of Andover Newton Seminary at Yale Divinity School

"In the time we live the need for spiritual discovery can seem overwhelming. Rev. Dr. Deborah Roof has superbly presented a courageous, engaging and unpretentious guide to help expand and deepen the reader's awareness of their own enduring threads of spiritual connection and love-centered faith."

—Thomas Warfield, Performing Artist, Director of Dance, NTID, Rochester Institute of Technology

This is one woman's story of faith, [...] d joy

"Deborah Roof had a mystical experience i[...] fter coming out as queer. She later lets God nudg[...] et of brown garb for a wardrobe splashy with tie[...]ell readers on the merits of church but tells the t[...] and more palpably–encounter the Divine outs[...]

This little book of wonders is ... for anyone who[...] Christian theology or just needs their longtime[...] the tender fresh skin underneath." —Molly Bask[...] pastor, author of *How to Begin When Your World is Ending*

"Roof's book presents an original framework for introspection on the daily life of faith." —Sarah Drummond, founding dean of Andover Newton Seminary at Yale Divinity School

"Engaging work, inviting us to reimagine our lives, and the church, as wondrous expressions of divine love—where God is still and always speaking!" —Anna Carter Florence, PhD, biblical scholar, Columbia Theological Seminary

"With humor and heart-filled honesty, the words of this beautiful book will instill wonder in your soul, ignite your spirit, and bring love to the center o[...] your life." —Karoline M. Lewis, PhD, biblical scholar, Luther Seminary

"There is a heart beating in Roof's new book. [Her] generosity with her own life invites readers to discover a spiritual core in their own experiences." —Maren C. Tirabassi, UCC pastor, author, poet

"A courageous, engaging, and unpretentious guide to help expand and deepen the reader's awareness of their own ... spiritual connection and love-centered faith." —Thomas Warfield, performing artist, direct[...] of dance, NTID, Rochester Institute of Technology

Peter E. Randall
PUBLISHER

SPIRITUALITY $14.9[...]
ISBN 978-1-942155-65-2

51495

9 781942 155652

thank you
for supporting my small business

No Exchange
Books
Religion &
Spirituality
savers

AO--AO-
283Y